# My Story—His Story

# My Story—His Story

## BY

## YOLANDA GLASS

☙❧

Edited by Kelly Taylor

# GLASS HOUSE PUBLISHING

Printed in the United States of America

ISBN: 978-0-9891093-0-7

Cover Design: Yolanda Glass

Cover Photography: Glenetta Glass

Cover Model: Gabrielle Glass

Learn more information at www.mystoryhisstory.com

*In loving memory of Dr. Lundy Savage.*
*I will never forget your encouraging words.*

# DEDICATION

I would like to dedicate this book to my father and mother, Pastor Louis and Juanita Barnes.  Thank you for never being afraid to be different and for encouraging me to do the same.


To my husband, Pastor Joe, and my children, Jorell (Glenetta), Janovia (Tremain), Raynard (Robyne), and Joe III.  I want to thank each of you for being the most wonderful family in the world to be a part of!  I am so grateful that the Lord allowed me to share this time and space on earth with you.


To my sisters, Ruebena and Vanessa, and, of course, my big brother Cleophus—I love you for all the great memories and for being a part of my life.


To my grandchildren: My prayer is that you come to love the Lord just as much as or even more than I do.

# CONTENTS

# INTRODUCTION

THIS IS NOT GOING to be an autobiography of my life but rather stories of actual events that happened earlier in my life, when I was between the ages of 3 and 6 years old. You may wonder, how can someone remember things in such detail at such a young age? I can't fully explain, but what I can tell you is that I have very vivid recollections of events from my early childhood. Later in life and over the years, when I recall these events to my mother and family members, they would awe and tell me there was no way I could remember these occurrences because I was only 3 or 4 years old at the time. My mother has openly wondered just how a child could remember such detail.

There was no doubt that my memories were accurate as I supplied details from our working-class neighborhood in a south suburb of Chicago, adequately named Chicago Heights. My recollections would often contain geographical evidence, such as the corner candy store and the nice storeowner who would challenge us to eat jalapeño peppers with the reward of a free gumball if we could endure the test. In the spring of 2011, just to be sure my imagination hadn't gotten the best of me, I visited the now blighted and abandoned area. Many of the landmarks are still standing—including Lincoln Elementary School, where I attended preschool, kindergarten, and first grade. I can still picture the department store in downtown Chicago Heights where I used to dream and beg my mom to buy one of the fancy dollhouses way up on the shelf, out of my reach, stocked with miniature doll furniture. *Oh, my! What I could do with a fancy dollhouse like that*, I would think. My mom, in true "we ain't got that kind of money" fashion, bought me and my sister little upholstered couches with tiny, removable cushions from the furniture collection instead.

Though at the time we weren't much aware of the racial climate that existed then in the early 1960s, I know now that my mother made a great sacrifice to buy us those doll chairs, as our dad was employed by the local steel mill. That steel mill was a black man's dream in those days, especially for a young man with a seventh-grade education fresh out of the Korean War by way of Mississippi.

I recall so much from this time period in my life that it seems implausible that a child could retain these events at such an early age. I watch my own grandchildren today and wonder just what they truly understand and whether they see life as vividly as I did. I am often reminded to be ever so cautious and mindful of my words and actions, knowing full well that the Lord has equipped and gifted many of our children to understand and discern events through their young eyes.

Granted, there are some things that are sketchy here and there; however, my mind has retained these mental mementos from a young child's point of view, with no conscious embellishments. I'm telling it to you just as I recall it.

### Where did all this happen?

I WAS BORN IN a Chicago suburb called Chicago Heights in the early 1960s. Okay, it was 1960—so now you know how young I am. My parents had one son and three daughters of which I am the youngest (or the "baby" of the family, as some would affectionately say). My mom, Juanita Barnes, was a homemaker, and my dad, Louis Barnes, migrated north from Mississippi to find work in the steel mills. Our neighborhoods were bustling and partially integrated. We attended school with White and Mexican children. From the time I could recall, life was interesting every day. The neighborhood was working class and diverse, ranging from the fathers like my dad who worked in the local steel mills to the occasional neighborhood drunk and fighting couples, but nothing that ever made us feel unsafe normally. Someone who may have been raised in a different environment may find it surprising that this setting did not seem threatening. It was far from Kansas—that's for sure!

Yet, I can honestly say we felt protected because it was a true neighborhood where neighbors cared for each other, and our parents, especially my dad, were always present to make us feel secure. There were times, however, that I received a glimpse of what the dark side of life must be like. I will share more on that later.

### What does my story have to do with His story? And, by the way, who is the "His" in "His Story?"

Over the years, in thinking over all the experiences in my childhood, I find that I have been able to glean important life lessons from each incident. I have used these lessons as wisdom markers, to forewarn my children and grandchildren of potential roadblocks and challenges in life. I've even used these experiences in teaching my Sunday school students throughout the years. These lessons have been used to understand that not only I but also others have vast life experiences that have shaped them as well, some of which are too horrifying to share on the pages of a book. Not that I don't have some of those, but I have not yet been compelled to share them on these pages at this time.

The *wisdom* of the lessons is how "my story" becomes "His story," the Lord's story that is. When I say the Lord, I am referring to my Heavenly Father, God, and the finished work of salvation that He has done in me through His son, Jesus Christ.

The scripture says the following in the book of Romans 8:28:

> *ȢAnd we know that all things work together for good to them that love God, to them who are the called according to his purpose.* (KJV)

When I accepted Jesus Christ as my personal savior many years ago, He took my life and He used all the broken pieces, even memories, times, and events up to that point and after, to make something useful, for Him. Thus, His purpose behind the events in my life translates into "His Story" of grace and incomparable love that is working every day of my life. I've found that when I look at each experience, I can now see God's hand teaching me and guiding me. Some of these slices of life are humorous when I recall them; others are disturbing but poignant and worth looking into. Come with me, dear friend, as my story becomes...

His Story.

PART I

# Decisions, Decisions

*᚛Wisdom is supreme; therefore get wisdom. Though it cost all you have, get understanding.*

*Proverbs 4:7* (NIV)

LIFE HAS A WAY of letting you know when you make a decision that probably wasn't so wise. Sometimes you will know instantly through painful correction whether you made a wise decision or not. Other times, you will find out later after going a great distance in the wrong direction. The stories that are to follow are some of my first recollections of making decisions that had an unexpected ending. We all have to make decisions in life, whether it be somewhat mundane decisions of what to eat or what to wear or more life-changing decisions

16

of who to marry or not marry, job and career choices, and so on. In my young mind, these stories served as the foundation for what not to do later in my life. I am so grateful that the Lord was with me when I did not have a clue where those decisions would take me.

# I Didn't Do It!

*ଔWisdom is the principal thing; therefore get wisdom: and with all thy getting get understanding.*

*Proverbs 4:7* (KJV)

ONE DAY, I CAME INTO the house from playing outside to find my mom in the kitchen as I normally would. As I approached the kitchen, I saw my mother standing at the sink. Just to give a little backdrop, my mom had just purchased a lovely new set of kitchen chairs—a set of six to be exact. We had gotten rid of the metal tube chairs that sported a blue, fake-marble print on vinyl. It was all the rage in those days—I'm sure. However, my mom, even on our modest budget, was able to purchase a brand-spanking new set of chairs. I'll never forget:

The vinyl color was a lovely modern rust color that didn't match a thing in the kitchen, but who cared! The legs and backs of the chairs were still like the old chairs, made of that '60s modern chrome tubing, but now we had sturdy backs and seats that were not worn or cracked like our previous chairs— flawless, at least until this day came. As I approached my extremely busy mother in the kitchen, I noticed that she was not smiling or as exhilarated as I was. One of the chairs was suspiciously moved to the center of the floor. Then I spotted it: a creative piece of ballpoint pen artwork scrawled, or I should say gouged, into the singled-out chair. I surveyed the "artwork" and instantly knew that these chairs did not come with any additional designs. I looked again at the artwork, then back up at my mother's unsmiling face, and then back to the artwork. Then the lesson began. As an adult, we've always joked as a family that my mom is an armchair psychologist. This story is full proof.

She began the conversation with me in the form of a question: "Yolanda, did you do this on purpose?" I was totally baffled. How much did she expect from a 4-year-old? My mind raced. *On purpose*? I was confused. *Hmmmm…on purpose*? Since she was waiting on an answer, I thought, *That must mean that I did not do it. Yeah, that's it! I did not do it…I didn't do it! Soooo, the answer will be yes*? After what was in my mind a successful thought process, I answered. "Yes! I did it on purpose!" The only thing I remember from that moment on was my other siblings surrounding me and the chair, gazing with convicting faces. I instantly knew that I had given the wrong answer to mom's diabolical question. I could also detect from the smirk on my sister's face that I had just become the scapegoat in a conspiracy.

I learned what that complicated phrase "on purpose" meant that day—maybe not in Webster's Dictionary terms but in terms that I would never ever forget from that day forward.

ᘉᘓᘔ

## My Story:

Lord, I was framed!

## His Story:

YOLANDA, YOU LACKED KNOWLEDGE, KIDDO.

ᘉᘓᘔ

Now come on—don't you agree that I was set up? No doubt they were waiting on my innocent little mug to come through the door. I smile a bit at the thought. The sight of me must have been a sure relief for someone in that room that day. Yet, if I look at this from God's word, my problem was that I was immature and lacked knowledge. My intellect had not developed to either answer my mother's question correctly or perhaps dodge the answer altogether. God's word states...

*ᘓMy people are destroyed for lack of knowledge.*

*Hosea 4:6* (KJV)

Just imagine all the pitfalls and pain we could avoid if we had better understanding and knowledge. Perhaps we're not too wise to think that we don't need to ask the Lord for more understanding. In the natural realm, you can increase knowledge and understanding by getting a quality education or even by becoming an avid reader. However, this scripture is referring to knowledge of the spiritual kind; although you can perish if you lack either, I feel it illustrates the knowledge and wisdom that only the Lord can give. How do you get it? You ask for it. I know that sounds very simple, but that is exactly what the word of the Lord states:

*℘If any of you lacks wisdom, you should ask God,*
*who gives generously to all without finding fault, and*
*it will be given to you.*

*James 1:5* (NIV)

Had I understood what the dreaded phrase "on purpose" meant that I had willfully scrawled on my mother's brand-spanking new dinette chair, I possibly could have been on guard and given my mother evidence that I had not been near or around that chair until the very moment of interrogation. Yet, fear and lack of knowledge on how to respond placed me in a position to be *destroyed*. The Word of God simplifies this even further by telling us how to get wisdom. Are you ready for the answer? Here it is:

*℘You want something but don't get it. You kill and*
*covet, but you cannot have what you want. You*

*quarrel and fight. You do not have, because you do not ask God.*

*James 4:2* (NIV)

If you need more wisdom in any area, just ask!

cͽ**Question:** What is it that you have not simply asked the Lord for today? No need to be "destroyed." The Lord is waiting on you to ask for the wisdom you need. It's just as simple as that.

# The Tricycle Challenge: Ouch!

*CST rust in the LORD with all your heart and lean not on your own understanding.*

*Proverbs 3:5* (NIV)

THIS STORY IS ONE of my earliest recollections of assessing a situation, weighing the risks, and making a decision. However, consequently, what a painful decision it was.

I was visiting my next-door neighbor's home. I was allowed to ride a red tricycle, which belonged to someone else. For some reason, I knew it was not mine. I recall riding the tricycle back and forth on a sidewalk that led from the back door to an adjacent driveway. I was undoubtedly enjoying myself immensely, as it was a warm summer day and I was able to ride that tricycle like the big kids! The back and forth journey must have become a little less adventurous for me because I began to go to the edge of the sidewalk that met the driveway. I would cycle to the very edge of the sidewalk and, by that time, skillfully reverse. After doing this a few times, I came right to edge of the sidewalk once again to survey just what was keeping me from riding on out into the driveway and on to many more riding adventures. I noticed that the driveway was not the same height as the sidewalk that I was riding on. Although I could not verbalize this, I knew there was a difference in height. I peered over the edge, giving this some thought. In my elementary-school mind, I thought about how I could navigate the drop-off at the end of the sidewalk, and here comes the fabulous decision-making process. I sat there momentarily and weighed my options. My imagination began to process my successful maneuver of the situation. I saw myself ride to the edge of the sidewalk, pedaling forward and the front wheel of the trike lowering gently onto the driveway and then the back wheels following in smooth pursuit. I would be home free to a much larger world of tricycling! Yes... I could do it! It was settled. I was going for it! Thus, with the vision in hand, I proceeded forward to my exciting destination. Having faith in my ability after that wonderful vision, I decided to pedal forward, or I should say *lunge* forward. To my horror, and before I could stop the disaster, momentum was working against me. My little frail body and the tricycle tumbled into the driveway chin-first. I can still see the concrete coming quickly toward my face! From a bystander's point of view, I went over a nearly 2-foot drop. The front wheel did not land smoothly, rather I did a nice somersault onto the concrete. It was more of an unplanned acrobatic move than the smooth ride that I had so vividly envisioned. As expected, I wailed in pain as I realized that my perfect plan not only ended my excursion that day but resulted in the most shocking pain. I ran home as fast as I could only to discover I had a silver-dollar-sized scrape on my chin—my only reward for careful planning that day.

 CB∞

# My Story:

I had a good plan, and it still resulted in disaster!

# His Story:

YOLANDA, YOUR WAY WAS NOT MY WAY.

I PROTECTED YOU ANYWAY.

CB∞

Many times we go on our way making plans for this and for that, and sometimes the outcome is nothing like we planned. As a matter of fact, you will find that not only is the outcome disappointing but even painful. "How could I have missed it?" you may have wondered. My experience with the tricycle was physical pain and an early lesson in failed physics. Certainly, I would never make such an unwise decision again. I knew for sure afterward that a 2-foot drop did not make for a happy transition on a tricycle. Likewise, there have been times in my life since that childhood mistake where I thought and was sure that I had made the right decision and was on course. Why? Because I had thought about it, weighed the pros and cons, and even envisioned just how it would turn out, only to have the result fizzle like a dull firecracker. In those times, I have to lick my wounds, get by myself, and ask, "Where did I go wrong, Lord?" Then, I have to admit that there was a point where a small doubt was there and my emotions took over. Perhaps visions of grandeur and acclaim overtook me, and I visualized myself with accolades or the praise of men. And oh how great it would be…for the Lord of course. This part actually brings what I call the *fear of God* upon me, only because it can be very dangerous to not heed the Lord's voice and *pedal* forward to disaster. Perhaps, He will have mercy on us and let us off with a scraped chin. How grateful I am to Him for scraped chins and not total disaster! It is a very humbling experience to find out that you can plan and figure all you want, but the Lord is going to have the last say. It is His distinction and His right as Sovereign Lord. I have to say also that, in simpler terms, He will not override His own laws of physics, reaping and sowing, and so on. You just can't go over a 2-foot drop in a tricycle and come out unscathed. Think about it.

CB80

CBQuestion: What natural or spiritual laws may you be attempting to override with your will? Take a step back and

26

carefully pray and seek Him before you pedal forward and go off of your own plans. You can be assured, it will be worth it.

಴ഔ

*಴Commit your actions to the LORD, and your plans will succeed.*

*Proverbs 16:3* (NLT)

# A New 'Do

*ஃHear instruction, and be wise, and refuse it not.*

*Proverbs 8:33* (KJV)

*I'm warning you, this story will give you a little chuckle at my expense. That's okay—God gets the glory!*

IT WAS A SPRING AFTERNOON—a warm Friday. I peered out the back door with my freshly washed hair, my dad and my uncle (my mother's brother) pulled into the backyard with a huge truck filled with dirt. When I first saw them drive up in the backyard, I bounded out of the back door with my newly washed and styled hair. I must take a sidebar here and explain a bit about my "hairdo." In case you're not aware, in the mid-1960s, African-American women went through a great deal—and still do to some extent—to make their hair *appear* manageable and acceptable. Please allow me to explain briefly:

My mother would ritualistically wash my hair on Fridays, and then early Sunday mornings at the break of dawn, she would sit me in front of the gas stove in the kitchen and press my hair with what we called a hot comb—and I do mean a *hot* comb. She used a special brass comb that was allowed to sit on the burner of the gas stove until it was red hot. She would then meticulously part my hair into manageable sections that were slathered with hair grease, a form of scented petroleum jelly, and pull the hot comb through each section of hair until it was bone straight. This ritual took place every week that I could recall of my childhood life. The results were stunning. We would get lovely curled bangs and hand-tied ribbons—not the ready-made barrettes and ribbons you see today. My mother would ask us to hold out our two index fingers so that she could use them to form the bows out of satin ribbon. Voila! Instant homemade hair accessories.

So, you're probably wondering what this has to do with the truck and the backyard. Well, the point is that when I walked into the backyard to meet my dad and uncle, I appeared with my freshly washed hair, which in my mom's eyes was just the beginning of her undoubtedly tedious weekly hair ritual (not just with me but my two older sisters as well). Now that we've pressed pause to get the hair background, let's press play to continue my story.

I walked around to the back of the truck to see that my dad and uncle were now standing in the back of the huge truck with what I thought were the largest shovels I had ever seen. They were standing in a huge mound of dirt. However, as I stood there, I noticed a distinct odor that did not come from normal dirt. It kind of smelled... really smelled. I didn't know my dirt varieties at the time, but I knew something was different. I watched as the men thrust in the shovels and cast the dirt from the back of the truck into a designated pile in the yard. Being the curious one, I got closer. My dad warned me to move back out of the way. I complied temporarily; however, I somehow moved back into the danger zone. Without notice, I suddenly glanced up to see what appeared to be a blur of dirt coming my way. I'm sure I was a sight, standing there with a heap of not only dirt but a good measure of cow manure covering me and my freshly washed hair! My uncle and dad could not stop laughing. "I told you to move!" my dad said through his laughter. I ran to the house screaming. I was a total mess, literally! What I didn't know was that the truck was filled with a fresh delivery of dirt mixed with dung! Now imagine my screams coupled with my mother's screams, knowing that she had to redo my 'do and wash out all that …er-um…doo-doo!

൬൭

## My Story:

Lord, I was just curious!

30

# His Story:

## YOLANDA, HE TOLD YOU TO MOVE!

ଔଚ୍ଚ

You may recall times in your life when you have the distinct feeling that it's time to "move." Whether it is moving from negative influences or bad habits, you get a nagging feeling that you should probably take action. Oftentimes, we will say to each other that "something told me" to do this or that, and we feel that we have a choice whether to obey that something. From my experience, if you're a Christian that something is, many times, the Holy Spirit leading you to His way and purpose. As long as we classify His voice as just something, I guess it's optional whether or not to take heed. But tell me, how many times have you ignored that *something* and run smack dab into a real problem? It may not be a pile of fertilizer on your head, but it stinks all the same. There you are, once again in the same old situation only because you are ignoring the warning to "move" before you experience a real inconvenience in your life.

My curiosity was more important to me at the time. I just had to get as close to the stinky situation as possible, even after I had been sufficiently warned. My need to be in the know was not as important as my well-being at the time. The command to "move out of the way" can come for several reasons. Sometimes your presence is not necessary to the advancement of the project. I know it's hard for some of us to believe, but here's a revelation: There are a lot of things that can get done much quicker if we are not in the way. For those of us who have to have control over everything in our realm, this may come as a shock. Another point is that you have a loving Heavenly Father who does not want you to get "dirty," so he lovingly warns you to "move out of the way." My dad was busy getting the work done, and there I was, standing in the way. Now, he wasn't going to stop the work, as much as he loved me. I could not see him saying, "Okay, Yolanda. You take as much time as you need to stare at us, and I tell you what, we will just do our best not get any dirt on you." It sounds silly, because it is silly to suggest that by our own will, we will come and go as we please and even "move" when we get good and ready. The Word of God says...

*Now listen, you who say, "Today or tomorrow we will go to this or that city, spend a year there, carry on business and make money.*

*Why, you do not even know what will happen tomorrow. What is your life? You are a mist that appears for a little while and then vanishes. Instead, you ought to say, "If it is the Lord's will, we will live and do this or that." As it is, you boast in your arrogant schemes. All such boasting is evil.*

*James 4:13–16* (NIV)

As grown and capable as we may be, we should not think that we alone have the power to make decisions for our lives, especially knowing our lives are not our own. The Lord's will is that we get to know Him well enough to hear Him when he says "move!" The next most important thing is to actually move when he warns. Otherwise, you will find yourself sporting a new stinky 'do that only His grace can wash out. Why bother? Just move!

ᛰᛰ

**ᛰQuestion:** What issues or circumstances should *you* "move" away from? Pray about it and ask the Lord for the courage and wisdom to move!

# PART II

# School Daze

*cȝWisdom is the principal thing; therefore get wisdom: and with all thy getting get understanding.*

*Proverbs 4:7* (KJV)

I ATTENDED PRESCHOOL, kindergarten, and approximately a month or two of first grade in Chicago Heights. I remember all of these experiences to some degree or another. The stories that I am about to share may seem to be a little scary from the point of view as a parent. However, you must know the mindset of this era. This was the early '60s, and having integrated schools was certainly not the norm. When I look back I wonder, although I don't know for sure, if race played a part in how we were treated at times. I was too young to decipher; however, I have distinct memories of incidents that

34

in hindsight I would question as a parent. Yet, in that time adults were not questioned, and tattling on an adult was considered totally disrespectful. There was an unspoken rule that if the teacher had to spank, which was totally legal and enforced, you would get another spanking when you got home. The teacher must be right! Even in these situations, the Lord was with me—protecting me. Not only did I learn my ABCs, but I got a good lesson in teachers-gone-bad and how even in that time, a life lesson could result.

The next three stories all come from my experience in the first grade. It was short-lived but filled with some very interesting experiences.

# Wrigley Spearmint, Anyone?

*CଷBlessed be God, even the Father of our Lord Jesus Christ, the Father of mercies, and the God of all comfort;*

*2 Corinthians 1:3* (KJV)

I CANNOT REMEMBER MY first-grade teacher's name. I just knew she was a White lady with a booming voice. All of her commands seemed to be shrill and forceful. She was much contrasted in comparison to my preschool teacher, who was so gentle and loving, or even my kindergarten teacher whose name was Mrs. Sun. Mrs. Sun was a chubby little lady who seemed to be bubbly and leaped around the classroom every day. My first-grade teacher was none of these by a long shot. I remember one day that I was sitting in the front of the classroom off to the left of the teacher's desk. I knew the rule was that you did not chew gum in her class. Somehow, I had secretly smuggled a stick of Wrigley Spearmint gum into class. I can see the white wrapper and silver foil now. The teacher was walking back and forth talking to the students. As she walked near the back of the class, I took my opportunity to carefully reveal the gum from its neat package and slip it into my mouth undetected. My mission was accomplished successfully. I savored the flavor of the gum as I chewed only at convenient intervals. My jaw would come to a complete halt as she came close to me. I was as attentive as ever. Nothing in my mouth…who me? Boy! How slick was I, fooling the teacher like that. However, I had a bad habit that would prove to unravel my plan that day. I liked to daydream on occasion. I guess the gum and the sights outside the window were just too much. I began to settle into a daze. Unbeknownst to me, as my teacher's voice faded into the background, my jaw began to move on its own. Instantly that loud booming voice was in front of my desk with an outstretched hand. "Give it to me!" she bellowed out. Stunned out of my euphoric daze, I stared at her hand. "Give me that gum!" she barked again. I gave up the gum that I was enjoying so intensely. Well, that was it. I was busted, and of course she would take my gum and tell my mother. Not a good day—but things got even worse! She took the gum and plopped it squarely in the front of my hair! I have a widow's peak, a simple little V-shaped point across my front hairline that I inherited from my mother, and for some reason, this was the prime target for the gum. To add insult to injury, she then proceeded to twist and intertwine my hair with the gum. After doing so, she advised me that that's what I got for chewing gum in her class and proceeded to sternly warn the entire class of my departure of the rules. As my heart sank, I could hear laughter. I wasn't listening before the gum placement, and I certainly did not hear another word she had to say afterward. I was thoroughly embarrassed. Lunchtime could not come soon enough. In those days, we walked home for lunch since it was a neighborhood school and most moms were home to prepare meals. As I made my way through the jeers to get my coat in the back of the room, my good friend, a little Mexican girl named Maria, consoled me. "Yolanda, I'm so sorry," she said. Her face was the only image of compassion in that heartbreaking moment. Her concern was my first memory of real compassion in a time of need.

CB80

## My Story:

Lord, I was humiliated.

## His Story:

YOLANDA, I SENT AN ANGEL TO COMFORT YOU.

CB80

I was guilty. I did it—I broke the teacher's golden rule to never chew gum in her class. I deserved punishment because I knew better. Even most of the children in the class agreed with their snickers that I was experiencing a deserved sentence for my actions. I got the whole package. Humiliation, guilt, shame, and to top it off, jeers, taunts, and condemnation.

I experienced this same exact feeling in my later years— the sin, then the guilt and shame, and on top of it all, the Devil telling me how stupid I was and how terrible I was. Who was I to argue? I did it. I broke the rule, and yes, I deserved every rotten consequence. Yet, just like my little friend Maria that day, the Lord sent a hand of grace my way, saying, "YOLANDA, I KNOW YOU SINNED, BUT I CARE ABOUT YOU SO MUCH THAT I WAS WILLING TO BE RIDICULED WITH YOU AND FOR YOU." That day at the coat racks, Maria took a chance to become unpopular along with me. In that crushing moment, the Lord sent an angel to comfort me and feel what I felt at that crucial time.

Have you ever had a moment like that? If you've ever had some kind of shame-filled experience, or even in the future if you find yourself overcome with shame as I was, there is a remedy. Jesus Christ experienced a moment of extreme compassion for *all* of our humiliation and guilt upon the cross. The book of Isaiah says…

*ଔBut he was pierced for our transgressions, he was crushed for our iniquities; the punishment that brought us peace was upon him, and by his wounds we are healed.*

*Isaiah 53:5* (NIV)

I believe He was saying, "I KNOW YOU'RE HURT VERY BADLY BECAUSE OF YOUR SIN, BUT I AM NOT HERE TO CONDEMN YOU—EVEN THOUGH I KNOW YOU'RE GUILTY."

*ଔTherefore, there is now no condemnation for those who are in Christ Jesus.*

*Romans 8:1*(NIV)

He came to bring us life and hope. When Jesus showed this compassion, he passed it on to us to allow us to be healed and to even heal others. Therefore, I can now be used to show compassion just at the moment when someone is walking through the jeers, taunts, and guilt of the enemy. He is there to let us know, "I'M SORRY DEAR ONE. I WILL BE WITH YOU IN YOUR SUFFERING."

ଔ୫ଓ

**ଔQuestion:** Have you ever had a time when the guilt and humiliation was overwhelming? Trust the Lord to heal you of that hurt and even send an angel to comfort you.

# Artists to the Gallows!

*When you pass through the waters, I will be with you; and when you pass through the rivers, they will not sweep over you. When you walk through the fire, you will not be burned; the flames will not set you ablaze.*

*Isaiah 43:2* (NIV)

I HAVE ALWAYS BEEN DRAWN to some form of art or craftwork for as long as I remember. Little did I know that this love would save me one day. On this particular day, the entire first-grade class was instructed to cut out and assemble an art project. The project consisted of fruit cut out of the appropriate colored construction paper arranged in a bowl. I cannot recall whether or not the fruit was cut out for us or whether we cut it out ourselves. I just remember that

41

afterward students were told to form a long line while holding their respective art projects. As the teacher began her review, I quickly realized that this was not a review for an accommodation or job well done. The line ended up being more like a fearful wait to see an evil Santa Claus. As each student approached her, she would take the project, examine it carefully, and give each an immediate, on-the-spot pass or fail. If it was a fail, the teacher's evil alter ego would emerge and begin screaming like a madwoman. I'm sure this may seem exaggerated, but I can only tell you what I experienced. There was one student that I'll never forget in the line that day; the girl was obviously not a good or great artist at age 6. After a quick glance, the teacher began to scream at the girl, citing her displeasure at her artwork. She then proceeded to get a firm grip on the young girl's hair from the right side of her head and punch the girl on the left side of the head with her fist. I recall the painful screams from the little girl as she sobbed away with her failed project.

That one scene added more terror and silence to the rest of us in the line. I was not far behind at this point and braced for certain death. You may recall, we would never complain to our parents about any abuse. We just thought that was the way it was. As I finally stood before the teacher, she looked over my artwork and said, to my utter shock and relief, "good." I was free to go back to my desk unharmed. I don't know if she smiled or not. I don't know if I smiled. I just know that I was very relieved not to be pummeled. I learned that day that I had something that would give me a "pass" with this teacher. I had an ability that allowed me to escape punishment. From that moment on, I can recall other projects that I made sure were perfect and done as instructed, and I was never unduly punished because of my gift.

CʒƧↃ

# My Story:

Lord, my artistic ability saved me from her
brutality.

# His Story:

YOLANDA, I GAVE YOU A GIFT TO COMPENSATE
IN YOUR TIME OF TRIAL.

CʒƧↃ

I once heard someone say that God gives you compensating gifts. Meaning, that if you have a disadvantage or disability of some sort that the Lord will make up for it by providing you with a gift or ability that will compensate or make up for your loss. That's what I experienced that day. Although, I was faced with a tyrant of a teacher who was out to find a reason to do unnecessary harm to the children in that room that day, I was given an out with my artistic gift. As I said earlier, in hindsight, I believe the teacher may have been brutal because so many of us were minority students. Considering the times, I think there was a good chance that my skin color was a problem to her, which became my disadvantage in her classroom. My only way of escape was my artistic ability.

The word of the Lord says…

> ℘When the enemy shall come in like a flood,
> the Spirit of the LORD shall lift up a standard
> against him.

*Isaiah 59:19b* (KJV)

That standard means that He will give you something to assist you just in your time of need. Just trust Him to do just that. There is another precious scripture that promises that the Lord will show you a way out of your trial or a way of escape! God's word makes it clear that every trial has a way out.

> ℘The temptations in your life are no different from
> what others experience. And God is faithful. He will
> not allow the temptation to be more than you can
> stand. When you are tempted, he will show you a way
> out so that you can endure.

*I Corinthians 10:13* (NLT)

What a loving God. If we trust Him, he will make a way for us to escape or get through our trials. That day I didn't know it, but I learned a very basic lesson. The lesson was that I was spared by my gift—my "way out." In other words, I was given a gift that "made room" for me. You may not be an artist, or you may not think that you have any special ability, but if you trust God, he will show you *your* personal "way out!"

*&A man's gift makes room for him and brings him before the great. Proverbs 18:16* (ESV)

On the issue of gifts or special abilities, don't despair by comparing yourself with someone else. As Romans 12:3 says, we have all been given a supply of faith by God. In other words, each and every one of us has something to work with. Sometimes, in this entertainment age, if we don't have a gift that is flashy or out front, we tend to take a back seat. I have some news for you: Everyone is someone in the Kingdom of God. Shall I repeat that? Everyone is someone in the Kingdom of God!

If you attend to God's word and place your life in His care through obedience and faith, your gifts will shine and come to the forefront. The things you thought you could never do will begin to blossom. Then suddenly, your life—just like my elementary artwork—will serve as a pass and a ticket to your peace from a world of tyranny. Your gift will even lead you to your purpose.

CB80

**CBQuestion:** What do you have in your hand that can serve as a gift in a time of distress or trouble? Not Sure? Just ask the Lord to show you. Trust that God will reveal that gift to you just when you need it. He is faithful.

# Free at Last,
# Free at Last!

*ℭ𝔰You will not fear the terror of night, nor the arrow that flies by day, nor the pestilence that stalks in the darkness, nor the plague that destroys at midday.*

*Psalms 91:5–6* (NIV)

As I STATED EARLIER, I do not recall my first-grade teacher's name, but I definitely knew of her demeanor and bad temper. So you can imagine the hope I received when I found out that my family was going to move out of the city to a little-known rural area 45 minutes south. Of course, at the time, I just knew we were moving and that we were packing all of our belongings into a big truck that was parked in the back of our home. My school was nearly a block away from where I lived. Actually, if you walked to the edge of the playground, you could see my backyard from there. One particular fall day, my day of deliverance finally arrived. We were playing on the playground when I saw my mother walking toward the playground from my house. My teacher was present with us as a group on the playground as she approached. If I were to describe what it was like to see my mother coming while I was in the presence of that teacher, it was like being rescued from a horrible captivity. The chain-link fence around the playground may as well have been iron bars! Mama arrived on the playground and announced to my teacher that she was there to get me so that we could leave and move away.

The most memorable part of this story was the absolute transformation that my teacher took on. I began to hear a kindness and sweetness in her voice that I never thought possible. Being on her best behavior, she said, "Class, Yolanda is moving today. We are going to miss her. Everyone say goodbye to her." As my mother took my hand and led me away, I was struck with the irony of my teacher's put-on in front of my mother. I also felt a bit smug that I got a chance to walk away from Her Evilness under the protection of my mom. I could hear as my class waved goodbye and called my name. Their voices sounded more like cries for help instead of well wishes. I waved goodbye and never looked back. I was free—at last!

 CR80

# My Story:

I never thought you would come, Lord!

# His Story:

YOLANDA, I MAY NOT COME WHEN YOU WANT ME TO, BUT I'M RIGHT ON TIME.

⋙⋘

There was a traditional saying in many African American churches when I was growing up, and still is today, that states, "He may not come when you want Him, but He's right on time." It speaks to the issue of God's timing in contrast to our timing. I'm sure all of us have been in a position where we felt that injustice was going unnoticed and it seemed like God was a silent bystander. His timing seemed to be off. Sometimes you can speak out with boldness and affect a change. Other times, you are forced to painfully observe while the evildoer seems to reign without accountability. Because of this, we get impatient for the answer. We sometimes wonder if God has an Out to Lunch sign on his door, or perhaps He's too busy dealing with the other billion or so people on the earth to notice. Numbers 23:19 says...

*⋙God is not a man, that he should lie; neither the son of man, that he should repent: hath he said, and shall he not do it? or hath he spoken, and shall he not make it good?* (KJV)

Now, the question is whether you believe Him or you don't—it's that simple. Yet, His word is sure and clear on the subject of holding all of us accountable for our actions. Hear what He says on this subject in Galatians 6:7:

> ☙Be not deceived; God is not mocked: for whatsoever a man soweth, that shall he also reap. (KJV)

In other words, if you plant corn, you will get corn—not tomatoes. In another place, the Word of the Lord states, in the book of 2 Peter 3:9...

> ☙The Lord is not slack concerning his promise, as some men count slackness; but is longsuffering to us-ward, not willing that any should perish, but that all should come to repentance. (KJV)

Basically saying, what we think is God's latency is really his perfect timing. I know it seems like evil has free reign in our lives and on earth sometimes, but rest assured, we serve a God that keeps a close eye on *everything*. As with any good accountant, you can best believe He will be sure that the books balance out one day. You may not be present to see it; often we would just gloat anyway. Just trust in His word and focus on what He has told you to do, and on that day when deliverance comes walking down the street to take your hand, you can just take her hand, walk away, and never look back! Glory to God! Say "hello" to Deliverance!

☙ജ

☙**Question:** What situation have you been worried about,

hoping that deliverance will come? Read Psalm 37 and then transpose that and read Psalm 73. Both chapters tell how the Lord will deal with those who seem to prosper in their evildoing.

Part III

# God Has a Plan

*⁣"For I know the plans I have for you," declares the*
*Lord, "plans to prosper you and not to harm you,*
*plans to give you hope and a future.*

*Jeremiah 29:11* (NIV)

MANY OF US CAN REMEMBER a time in our lives when calamity and even certain danger came upon us. The mere fact that you are able to read this tells me you were able to escape somehow, some way. I've heard some say that when someone is able to thwart the hand of death, it is taken to mean that an individual was given another chance at life. It is often said that God must have a plan for him or her—to have been spared in such a way. I have three such incidents that I experienced as a child. Not that I haven't had many rescues of grace since then, but it's these occurrences in particular were burned upon my memory, leaving a permanent negative that has developed into a live film that plays upon recollection. Did God have a plan? I believe so. And since I believe He is God, I also believe He is the creator of everything else, the earth, and mankind. Just based on that, He definitely knows what He's doing. So in my finite way of thinking, that must mean that everything is part of a larger plan, and somewhere in there, I must play a part. Without getting philosophical, I can only say that I'm still here to write this, so perhaps my being able to share this with you is part of the overall plan. One thing is for sure: Had I not survived, these pages would be blank.

# I Believe I Can Fly

*CßAnd I said, Oh that I had wings like a dove! for then would I fly away, and be at rest.*

*Psalm 55:6* (KJV)

WHEN I WAS YOUNG, I loved the smell of my mom's hands whenever she helped me to get dressed in the morning. They had a fresh and familiar scent—an indescribably clean scent specific to her—as they busied themselves at combing my hair or buttoning my shirt. I can remember the deliberateness with which those hands speedily accomplished the task. The memory is clear in my mind. One morning (at least it felt like a morning), my mom gave me a gown to wear. Now, my adult mind is saying, *why would she put a gown on you in the morning?* As I said, my childhood memory says it was morning, so I am going to stick with that. The gown was white and had a special feature: On the shoulders were little triangular flaps that extended from each shoulder. There was writing on the front of the gown. My mother told me that it said Angel. She went on to explain to me that the flaps were wings. My imagination took it from there. I recall my thought sequence going something like, *angel, wings, angel, wings.* Somehow the thoughts moved on to *wings, fly, you, wings...fly!* I was fascinated by my newly acquired potential to fly. So you may be wondering what I did at this point. You may have guessed—I wanted to try them out.

In the backyard, we had an old shed, of which I never really knew what was inside. I just know that my dad would go back and get stuff out of there now and then. There was a ladder leaning against it. The shed had a flat roof and in human height was definitely not larger than our house, so I wandered out there and began to climb. I reached the top of the shed and crawled on top. I noticed that there was old, dried paint spills everywhere in solid puddles. The color orange is what I recall. I stood up and looked back toward the house. There I was, off the ground and poised to take flight. I stood confidently and walked toward the edge. When I looked down, a healthy fright came over me. My faith in those little flaps on my gown suddenly took flight. The truth of my situation came to light. I was on a roof at least 8 feet from the ground and I could not fly! To top things off, I couldn't figure out how to get back on the ladder and go down the way I came. The problem was that I could not see the ladder from that vantage point. I could see the ground, the back of my house, and the sky. I begin to cry and call for my mother. I recall feeling as if I was on that roof for an entire day. This, of course, is likely not true when I look back on that now. I kept calling and crying out for someone to rescue me. I do not remember who eventually heard me and came outside. I just recall it was a male, and he asked me how I got up there. I was a blubbering mess by then and just wanted to get down. Even if I did have wings, they did not serve me well that day.

⊂ঙ৪৩

## My Story:

Hooray! I got a new name and wings to boot! I can fly!

## His Story:

THE TITLE AND THE WINGS ARE A GIFT, BUT I'LL TELL YOU
WHEN YOU CAN FLY.

⊂ঙ৪৩

I have had times in my life where I get this certain boost of confidence and I launch into an idea or event—knowing that it's going to be a success—only to find out later that I might have misjudged the timing and even my current ability for the task. Ultimately, the whole thing falls apart. So what do I do when I get up there, trusting in fake wings? I cry out! "Lord, please help me to get down off of this stupid roof! I thought I had wings, and now I've found out that not only can I *not* fly but that I have gotten myself into a real pickle here!" I begin

55

to cry out, "Help! Mama! Help! God! Help me!" I go on for what seems like forever. Does He show up? Oh yeah, He shows up every time to help me and get me out of danger. There I am, crying and blubbering something like,"I thought I had these wings, and I found out that they were not real when I climbed up on the….and I got scared and…whaaaaa!"….and so on.

Often in response, He speaks to my heart saying, "HOW DID YOU GET UP THERE? C'MON, LET ME HELP YOU DOWN DAUGHTER." Once again, I'm safe in His arms. So what's the lesson? I guess if I could glean anything, I would say, just because you're wearing a gown that says "angel" and a set of fabric wings does not mean that you will be able to defy the law of gravity and begin to fly. You are in a human body right now. I know the songs says, "One glad morning, I'll fly away," but not just yet. And if you get yourself in a mess, thinking you can fly with man-made wings, call Him and He will come and rescue you. I know He's done it for me many times over.

ॐ

ॐ**Question**: What things are you jumping to conclusions on? Are you stuck on the roof of unrealized expectations, abilities, and hopes?  Dear one, I love the fact that God is a loving God and cares for us. Don't be ashamed if you've found yourself on the "roof" of false hopes.  Call him today. He'll come and get you Himself.

ॐ

*He shall call upon me, and I will answer him: I will be with him in trouble; I will deliver him, and honour him.*

*Psalm 91:15* (KJV)

# I Am Blind—I Can't See!

*❧He rebuked the Red Sea, and it dried up; he led them through the depths as through a desert.*

*Psalm 106:9* (NIV)

GROWING UP IN Chicago Heights was far from any country living. We lived in a city, a suburban city, and it was all concrete and sidewalk. Everywhere we went we had to cross a street to get to the corner store, to school, or to our aunt's house.

One particularly sunny day, I was hanging out with my sister Vanessa and my two older cousins, Collette and Bobbi Jo, who were sisters. It was very common for us to play games that were accompanied by rhythmic songs and cadence. It was a daily game in the summer to sing, "Miss

Mary Mack, Mack, Mack…all dressed in black, black, black…with silver buttons, buttons, buttons…all down her back, back, back!" Another game we would play was, "O' Sailor." Two of us would face each other and perform a coordinated series of clapping each other's hands while we sang, "O' sailor went to sea, sea, sea to see what he could see, see, see! And all that he could see, see, see was the bottom of the deep blue sea, sea, sea!" We would make hand gestures to symbol everywhere that the sailor went. We even made up some places along the way. On this day, we made up a song and a little game called, "I am blind—I can't see." Yes, that was it. I know it sounds profound, but let me continue with this ingenious game. We locked arms and proceeded to walk all around the neighborhood with our eyes (get this) closed. So there we were, walking like enlisted soldiers singing in unison, "I am blind! I can't see! If I knock you down, don't you blame it on me!" We even had a little Supremes kind of tune to it. As far as I can remember, we made this little rhyme up that very day!

We sang and marched blindly, smiling and singing. We then came to a very busy street that we needed to cross. It seemed like hundreds of cars were on the streets. We knew this street was different because it had four lanes to cross to get to the other side. I now know it was a four-lane street called Lincoln Highway, or what most nowadays would call Route 30, which was a main thoroughfare through Chicago Heights toward Indiana. To this day, this route is still extremely busy, and for sure, we had no business trying to cross it. As we marched on up to the curb singing our song, we all paused with eyes now open, trying to figure out how we could all get across together. My cousins and sister were all at least 2–4 years older than I was, with none of us being older than 9 at the time. Someone said, "Okay, when I say 'go,' everybody run!" Before I could process the strategy, they had all taken off running. My hand came loose from one of them as they darted across what seemed to be a massive expressway. I could see their backs as they were running. I got a delayed start in an effort to catch up. Everything goes in slow motion from here. I made it across the first westbound lane, and just as I was crossing the next one, I froze. I could see a powder-blue-colored car coming toward me. I could not move. My feet were cemented to the pavement. The next thing I heard was the screeching of tires and car brakes, and the hood of the car stopping at an arm length in front of me! I could not move—I was in shock. The driver began to yell and curse at me. What's funny is that I don't recall seeing the driver, just hearing the fury in his voice. I'm sure I was a sight with probably the most stunned look on my face. It seemed as if all the traffic noises had stopped for me in all directions. I turned to see my sister and cousins standing on the curb across the street with their eyes and mouths wide open. No longer blind, obviously. With traffic at a standstill, and with all the adrenaline and fear I could muster, I was able to run across the street in Red Sea fashion.

As I mounted the curb, I could hear my sister and cousins yelling and asking me why didn't I keep up with them. I'm sure I did not have the intellect to explain why that was my fault. I just knew in my young heart that I had escaped something terrible, and all the singing and games in the world could not erase that horrifying experience.

CRSO

## My Story:

They left me. I wasn't ready to run!

## His Story:

YOLANDA, I KNOW YOU TRIED, YET MY ANGELS WERE PROTECTING YOU ONE MORE TIME.

CRSO

Have you ever tried to keep up with someone who seemed way ahead of you? There you were, in a position of weakness or inadequateness, yet you try to run with them anyway. Instead of following your God-given instinct to stay put, you follow them, and it happens: You almost meet sudden disaster because of it. In my case, the Lord, knowing my inability, stepped in and added His ability to my inability. He helped me. He protected me in my state of weakness. Surely I could have stayed back, but I wanted to be with the group, singing, laughing, playing, and having fun. I wanted to be a part of them—walking in cadence, belonging with them. Yet, I was not supposed to move just then. I should have waited and risked the fact that they would have called me weak for staying back—even risk the ridicule of not being fast enough to keep up, hearing, "C'mon...let's go! What's wrong with you?" What I heard was, "You almost got yourself killed because you are weak!" The reality was that even though no one looked back to make sure I was safe, as children would do, the Lord made sure He was there. He stopped all the traffic so that I could cross over safely.

Life will get you out in the middle of the street and let your hand go. There you are, unchained from a helpful human hand. You can't go forward, and you can't go backward, so you freeze. You suffer depression and sadness, not making any progress. Why? Maybe because you think it's your fault that you weren't fast enough to run out of your situation. You almost got yourself creamed. Just then, in the midst of accusations from the enemy and the risk of all ridicule, He stops everything, and if you look forward, you will see you can now safely pass.

Your personal Red Sea has opened up right before you. Just look up.

Listen, I have a Word for you today: The Lord Jesus is getting ready to stop all the madness and make a way for you!

> *Behold, I will do a new thing; now it shall spring forth; shall ye not know it? I will even make a way in the wilderness, and rivers in the desert.*
>
> *Isaiah 43:19* (KJV)

ɔʒ℘

**Question:** In what areas of your life do you feel frozen? Are the taunts and accusations of the enemy ringing in your ears, paralyzing you? List those things and take them to the Lord in prayer. Then, with His ability, get back up and start running, and He will stop all traffic—just for you!

# Start Kickin'

*Now there were four men with leprosy at the entrance of the city gate. They said to each other, "Why stay here until we die?*

*2 Kings 7:3* (NIV)

THE HOUSE THAT I have the most memories of in Chicago Heights is the house on Wallace Street. I remember that there was a Wonder Bread decal on the front window of the house. That's because, according to my parents, a previous owner used the front portion of the house as a general store. I always think of the house as having two living rooms: one in the front where the store used to be, sort of like a front room, and the other near the back of the house where the television and couches were. We did not spend much time in the front room.

It seemed empty to me. Very little furniture was stored in the room, only a chair here and there and an old refrigerator on dark hardwood floors. I can remember us opening up the door of the refrigerator and seeing a light come on; however, it was never cold, and there was never any food kept in it. One particular afternoon when my Aunt Anna Dora, my mom's sister, was babysitting us, I wandered from the back living room to the front room where the old fridge was. In that day, the freezer was on the bottom of some models and opened with a separate door. I opened up the bottom door and examined it. There wasn't a light in the bottom as it was in the top. I could see the perfect hiding place, and somehow, I knew I could fit in there. Going back to my tricycle reasoning, which I illustrated in an earlier story, I tested the door. I wondered if I could get out. I opened and closed the door several times from the outside and saw that the door opened and closed with ease. Now that I am an adult, I suppose the fact that I had to test was evidence of an unexplained apprehension. After my little test, I proceeded to crawl inside with my back first in a fetal position. I closed the door and enjoyed the feeling of hiding where no one could find me. After a little bit of time, I decided it was time to come out and gave the door a push. It did not open. Again, I pushed—nothing. Next, I kicked. It didn't budge. Keep in mind that I am curled up in this little box that presented a challenge to doing either, yet, I gave it all I had. I kicked and screamed and pushed. As my family has told it, my aunt noticed that I was not with the other kids and came looking for me. Everyone was looking all over the house trying to find me. My aunt said that when she came to the refrigerator she could hear this thumping noise. She then opened the door, and I came tumbling out! I have since heard many a story of how children have suffocated from playing hide-and-seek in old refrigerators and freezers. Not knowing that the magnetic strip that allows the door to shut snuggly also creates a vacuum from the inside that cannot be not be broken by a child. I did not have much time or oxygen left when my aunt opened that door. I was certainly only a few breaths away from unconsciousness and death. If I had not kicked and screamed…you know the rest.

C33EO

## My Story:

Help!

## His Story:

I HEARD YOU!

C33EO

What can I say? He saved me! If I had gone to sleep, I would have died. If I did not try to get out, my aunt would have never heard me. There's a story in the bible in 2 Kings Chapter 3 where two men knew that they were certain to die in an imminent invasion by the opposing enemy. They discussed their plight with each other and decided, "Why stay here until we die?" They decided to get up and go into the city that night and surrender in hopes that they would secure some kind of mercy from the enemy's camp, thus taking an extreme risk that they could die anyway. In other words, they made a move. They "started kicking!" They did not just sit there and accept death. They did something, and you know what? When they moved, the Lord magnified the sound of their movements to the point that the enemy thought they were being overtaken and fled! Now, here are two guys entering an empty city with pots on the stoves, cattle in the fields—all free for their taking! They did something when faced with the inevitable. The Lord used them in their moving, or as I would like to say, their *kicking*. In the same way, the Lord allowed my frantic kicking to be magnified in my aunt's ears that day. I was rescued from death because I put up a fight. What am I trying to say? Don't just sit there and accept the inevitable. Yes, it looks grim, but if you can move your pinky toe, get to moving! The Word says to resist the Devil, and he will flee! Maybe, just maybe, if you exerted some effort rather than just sitting there and taking it, you would get a surprising outcome.

ᆼᄋ

**ᆼQuestion**: In a tight spot? Looks like the end? Have you screamed and kicked yet? If you don't move, neither will God.

Part IV

# Battle Scars

*He heals the broken hearted and binds up their wounds.*

*Psalm 147:3* (NIV)

THE FOLLWING EXPERIENCES were not so pleasant. I feel as though the Lord has walked and worked me through most of this and healed my heart on these issues. However, I must confess, this has been one of the hardest parts of the book to touch. I was almost finished, and as I looked at my notes, I could see that I was getting to the part of the book that would cause me to have to resurface some painful events. I would like to be able to say that the only thing left is the scars from the wounds in my soul, but I have to be honest—I often wonder how much of me today is acting out from the me of yesterday. I may never know. Yet, I want to share because I know there are many out there just like me hiding extremely painful times behind bright smiles and elegant clothing in an effort to conceal the rejection of a world that is blighted by the curse of sin. I pray that my experience will illustrate how God can heal the hurt—even if a scar remains.

# Internal Wounds

*ℂℨMy God, my God, why hast thou forsaken me? Why art thou so far from helping me, and from the words of my roaring?*

*Psalm 22:1* (KJV)

As I STATED EARLIER, my mom would put myself and my sisters through a weekly ritual of washing our hair on Friday's and hot pressing our hair early on Sunday mornings. One particular Sunday morning, I was outside of our house on Wallace Street waiting my turn to get my hair pressed. There was a light pole right in front of our house. It was one of those light poles that had a thick cable running diagonally from the lower portion into the ground. The thick steel cable was covered with a galvanized casing. We, or at least I, would go outside and twirl around this portion of the cable for fun. Fun was kind of hard to come by in those days, I suppose. As I held on to the cable this particular morning with my head back to the sky, a young black man, perhaps in his late teens or early twenties, came by. I recall very vividly that he had on a brown tweed cap. I would call it a brownish herringbone tweed cap. He came up to me as I was twirling in my own world. I noticed that he was smoking a cigarette. Before I could figure out what he wanted, without notice, he snatched me up by my left arm and extinguished his cigarette on my young shoulder. I screamed with anguish as he ran away. My young mind did not know how to comprehend what or why this happened. My mother appeared at the door quickly when she heard me yell. I was crying incomprehensively. Her face was one of anger and disappointment, which confused me even further. She asked me what was wrong, so I tried to blubber out what happened while pointing to my arm. My mother pulled me into the house and chided me for being out there alone. Today of course, I do not blame her, as I realize she must have been frustrated. I am also sure had my father known or been there, he would have taken care of the situation—being the fierce provider and protector that he was. However, I somehow internalized that I was certainly to blame for what happened, and no one was going to be my hero that day and try to find the guy who did this to me. From this incident, I began to believe that something about me must have been extremely ugly and bad enough for this stranger to inflict such abuse upon me.

# My Story:

I must have been pretty hideous looking for this man to abuse me in such a way.

# His Story:

I WANT TO HEAL YOU FROM THAT HURT. YOU ARE MADE IN MY IMAGE, AND I LOVE YOU. YOU ARE MY PRECIOUS DAUGHTER.

C3 ∞

I still have a small circular scar on my left arm from that day. It was on my upper shoulder when I was a child, but as I grew it moved to the top of my shoulder and is almost unnoticeable today. That's a good thing, because I have successfully blotted this event out of my conscious memory. But what about my soul? I can feel the sadness and shock as I reminisce. However, there is a part of me that does not feel so ugly anymore. How did this healing happen you may ask? I can't exactly recall when, but it was several years ago when the Lord brought this incident to my memory. I call it "bubbling up." Usually, when the Lord wants to deal with something and heal it within me, He will allow the experience to bubble up to the surface of my remembrance. I felt the Lord speak to me about this. He showed me that it was not my fault that this guy did this to me. I realized that this incident had affected how I saw myself. I felt unattractive and ugly and even reprehensible. Why me? Why did he do such a mean thing to me? Was it because he thought I was just so ugly that he could not stand the sight of me? I often wondered. Yet, I never knew these thoughts were buried in my heart until the day the Lord brought this from deep inside of me. I later realized that the enemy had used the pain, as he often does, to plant a seed of inferiority and lack of self-confidence in me. Over time, my Heavenly Father began to let me know just how much he genuinely loved me. He did this in so many ways, and still does, in ways that only He and I know. Whether it's having someone give me something that only the Lord knew I wanted, or allowing me to come across a rare item that was a deep desire for me. He will even work something out for me that only He can do. When I see these signs of love, I smile knowing that He's with me. He compensates for all the hurt and pain. His goodness toward me has filled up the hole where the pain was. There is a scripture (Psalm 45:13) that the Lord has allowed me to use over the recent years that states…

*The King's daughter is all glorious within…*(KJV)

Through these words, I am able to visualize what a King's daughter must feel like. The honor she reflects because of *whom* her Father is—the King! Her garments, her countenance, and even her walk are self-assured with nobility and dignity in every step. No heads hanging down, no drooping of her shoulders, but a true princess—made from royalty, feet made only to walk in royal palaces of marble and light! You want to know something? That's how the Lord sees you and me. This is not just for when we get to heaven, but this is for right now. If you can see yourself the way the Lord sees you (lovely, righteous, and truly *His*) you will allow him to heal you. You will begin to walk like a royal princess! Shoulders squared with a knowing smile—that somebody unquestionably loves you!

ϹϾ

**ϹϾQuestion:** What things have you repressed that the Lord may want to bubble up to the surface for healing? Don't dwell on the past but be open when the Lord brings things to your mind over time for healing. When you're ready, He will apply his healing balm to the wounds. Not only that, He will continuously remind you of His love every day—if you let Him.

ϹϾ

*ϹϾThe LORD hath appeared of old unto me, saying,*
*Yea, I have loved thee with an everlasting love:*
*therefore with loving-kindness have I drawn thee.*

*Jeremiah 31:3* (KJV)

# Don't Let the Devil Ride

*osNeither give place to the devil.*

*Ephesians 4:27* (KJV)

Our NEIGHBORHOOD TEEMED with an array of nationalities and children from diverse backgrounds. For instance, I had a good friend at school, a little Mexican girl named Maria. Our neighbors were Mexican and showed us how they made flour tortillas directly on the burners of their gas stove. We were also friends with some White children down the street. One of the boys died young, which was terribly painful to us. Every day was loud, with double-dutch jump rope, hopscotch games, and friends from all walks of life. Therefore, it was no big deal for us to visit our neighborhood friends' homes and for them to visit ours. Mom didn't like it, but we would sneak over to each other's homes to play with toys or listen to someone play the record player.

One particular day, our neighbor's adopted son, Duane, came over while my mom and dad were gone. My oldest sister Ruebena watched us at times when mom and dad were away for short periods of time. Duane was what we called a "bad" boy. He was a bully, and usually when he was around, someone was going to end up in tears. Duane came over and was playing around and asked me did I want to play horsey. He said I would not get hurt and got down on all fours and said, "C'mon... I won't hurt you." He smiled, and I climbed onto his back grasping the back of his shirt as reigns. He began to gallop around the living room. I could hear my sisters and my brother laughing as I was experiencing what was more like a bull ride than a horsey ride. As he was making a final pass in and around the living room furniture, he stopped abruptly in front of our black-and-white console television set. In those days, there was no such thing as a childproof home. Everything had sharp corners or it would not have been the most fashionable furniture. My out-of-control pony paused quickly in front of the television set and bucked violently enough to send me flying right into the sharp corner of the television console. I flew into a fit of tears as I emerged with blood trickling down over my left eye from a gash on my forehead. I still sport the remnants of that scar today. Being our protector, my sister Ruebena panicked and began to yell at Duane. He pushed her and ran out of the house. In recollection, we did not feel safe in our own home. This person had done something evil and left (in a good mood actually) with no remorse. I remember my sister tying an old chintzy nylon scarf around my head to bind the wound. I can now understand why my dad was in such shock when he came home. There I was with a bloody scarf over my head and left eye. What a mess! My dad immediately went next door and reported the issue to Duane's mom. We didn't get to witness it personally, but the word on the street was that he experienced a lot of physical pain behind that one.

CʒƧʘ

## My Story:

How could so much fun go so wrong?

## His Story:

DON'T LET THE DEVIL RIDE.

CʒƧʘ

"Don't let the Devil ride?" What in the world does that mean? When I was young, there used to be an old Bluesy gospel song called "Don't Let the Devil Ride." The songster would say, "Don't let the Devil ride. If you let him ride, he will want to drive. Don't let him ride." We used to hear the old quartet groups sing it at church. In other words, don't let the Devil (a.k.a.) Satan in or he will surely cause trouble. The trouble can only come in because you "let him ride." In my case, I was offered to take a ride from someone with wrong motives. Our neighborhood bully was known for his malicious acts long before we let him into our house that evening. He came in playful and not appearing to do harm.

77

Once he got in, he was set to do damage, and he did. None of that would have happened had we obeyed our parents and not let him into our home while Mom and Dad were out. His reputation certainly preceded him, and we knew he was far from a friendly playmate. I'm sure there may have been times when you were trusting of someone that you found did not have your best interest at heart, or you tried something that you thought you were strong enough to resist. We opened the door and the worst happened. The person or the temptation, while soothing or pleasurable at first, began to take over and drive us to places of wrong relationships, addictions, and pain—all because we let him ride. God's Word gives clear warning on temptation and dealing with the enemy of our souls in Ephesians 4:27:

*csNeither give place to the devil.* (KJV)

Our problem is that we often allow temptation to come in. Just a little more pushback and Satan will back off. The word of God says...

*csSubmit yourselves therefore to God. Resist the devil and he will flee from you.*

*James 4:7* (KJV)

Today's society, at times, has bought into the lie "the Devil made me do it." This lie originated in the garden with Eve. The even bigger delusion is that Satan does not exist. I hold the belief that if one believes there is a God in Heaven, there must also be a corresponding belief of an opposing force called evil. We may not want to appear spooky or seem too primitive in our evolved society; however, make no mistake about it—evil is real. The Devil is real, not just in the lowest and criminal places but also in high places of apparent success in the form of greed, pride, and complacency.

The truth is, once we look too long, gaze too much, and consider sin in our hearts for too long, we are leaning toward situations with an adverse outcome. It does not matter what neighborhood or conditions you come from, everyone is fair game to the enemy of our soul. At risk of preaching a little bit, the last place you want to be is in the aftermath, holding your head, unsteady and wounded. Don't let him ride.

CR80

**Question:** Have there been instances when you've gotten relaxed and trusted in the wrong people or the wrong things? Are you still tempted by a little bit of sin? Remember: The enemy wants it all, not just a little. I'll say it one more time...don't let him ride.

CR80

*Don't you realize that this sin is like a little yeast that spreads through the whole batch of dough?*

*1 Corinthians 5:6b* (NLT)

# DON'T LET THE DEVIL RIDE

(Public Domain)

Don't let the Devil ride

Oh don't let the devil ride

'Cause if you let him ride

He'll want to try to drive

Don't let him ride


Don't let him flag you down

Don't let him flag you down

If he flags you down

He'll turn your soul around

Don't let him ride

Don't let him be your boss

Don't let him be your boss

If you let him be your boss

He'll make your soul be lost

Don't let him ride


Don't let him ride with you

Don't let him ride with you

If he ride with you

He'll tell [you] what to do

Don't let him ride

❧

Part V

# Cover Judging

*Do not judge others, and you will not be judged.*

*Luke 6:37* (NLT)

*I realize that the placement of this section is a little odd. There is actually only one account in this chapter. I originally took it out, and just before I ended the book, things didn't feel right. The book seemed incomplete without it. So here it is in a section all its own.*

I LEARNED EARLY ON as a little child how you can misjudge someone by their actions or appearances. As the saying goes, never judge a book by its cover. It's a lesson that I have had to learn over and over until this day. God's love is unconditional, which is quite hard for us to believe at times. His word, in Matthew 5:45, says that He "sends rain over the righteous and the unrighteous." (NIV) Unlike many of us as well as society, He also doesn't play favorites.

> ☙Then Peter replied, *"I see very clearly that God shows no favoritism."*
>
> *Acts 10:34* (NLT)

As much as we would like to think so, He does not prefer any of us to the other. That's something that we as humans came up with. Here is one such account where I learned this lesson in an interesting way.

Y OU MAY HAVE ALREADY figured out why my parents decided to move us out of the city when I was in first grade. Chicago Heights held within it some pretty fascinating characters.

One day, my oldest sister, Ruebena, and I were sitting on the front steps of our house. There was a woman passing by who was obviously extremely inebriated, or I should say drunk. She staggered along as my sister and I observed. Just as she approached the sidewalk in front of our house, she dropped her purse of which all the contents came pouring out. The thing that got our attention was the money that was lying all over the place. There was enough change to make a kid quite happy at the penny candy store. I don't recall my sister saying anything to me or vice versa. I just recall that we looked at each other when we saw the money. It was a knowing look that hoped this woman's stupor would net us some coins that day. We watched as she stooped down mumbling and grappling for her purse and all its contents. Note that we were not offering to assist her with her task. Little by little, she picked up each item, retrieving it and putting it back into her purse. Eventually, she cleared the sidewalk of each and every item. Even the stray pennies and dimes that had rolled away from her were gathered up. Once she completed her task, she was back on her way, meandering down the street.

We could not believe our eyes. How could someone who could barely walk or even think clearly be that accurate? When I was older, I understood that having one's capacity impaired did not necessarily mean that there wasn't a wise person in there. We were majorly disappointed, as we didn't get a free trip to the candy store that day.

C8**ॐ**80

# My Story:

The lady didn't leave us a dime!

# His Story:

NEVER JUDGE ANOTHER MAN'S SERVANT.

C8**ॐ**80

Let's go on and admit it: Sometimes we may look at someone on the outside or how they are behaving, and we instantly size them up. You know the drill—we figure out their intelligence level right away or even on a spiritual plane, we determine their net worth in terms of what *we* can see. Other times, we may take out our measuring tapes and begin to size up their economic or educational status. When we are enlightened or given understanding, we can forget how it was before we were given wisdom.

Oftentimes, what we don't see is that God has given *everyone* a gift or talent that may go unnoticed. Just because someone exhibits a particular behavior does not necessarily mean that they don't have insight or understanding in many other areas. I have had marked experiences where the Lord has used people who, in my narrow-mindedness, I thought were of lesser value to offer me blessings or tell me about a dream they've had to give me insight. The Lord has taught me that He can use whomever He wants, and that I, as a Christian, may want to be a little more careful in how I size people up, not forgetting the hand of mercy that gave me a new life.

*ↄ3Who are you to judge someone else's servant? To his own master he stands or falls. And he will stand, for the Lord is able to make him stand.*

*Romans 14:4* (NIV)

On the flip side, have you ever had situations where you could see the look on people's faces, seemingly waiting for you to make a mistake so that they could take advantage of your impairment—not considering that there was a soul behind your eyes or even a wisdom that was not apparent? If you are someone that has been misunderstood along the way and not heard, please be encouraged. All is not lost. Take heart—Jesus was judged wrongly, yet he was able to complete his mission and provide us with salvation. Just know that the Lord is able to make you stand in the midst of all the accusations.

I also have to remind myself that we are all in certain stages of spiritual growth and that where someone is struggling today may not be the case tomorrow. After all, the good news is that God is able to make him or her stand. Regardless of what things look like on the outside or what you and I may think, God's love is still there looking at the heart and not just looks.

*The LORD doesn't see things the way you see them. People judge by outward appearance, but the LORD looks at the heart.*

*1 Samuel 16:7* (NLT)

❧❧

**Question**: Who have you sized up and looked down upon in your life? First of all, let's ask the Lord to forgive us and then ask Him to show us how to better approach those individuals with humility and respect.

❧❧

**Second Question:** Have you been personally discouraged by being misunderstood or your intentions misjudged? Please remember, God loves you unconditionally—no matter what others may think or say.

# My Story—His Story

C3॰80

## My Conclusion

Over the years, I have recalled these stories along with others in humor and, in some cases, somberness. Looking back, I can see God's hand of mercy and grace over my life. He has allowed me to survive until this day, as I continue to experience His hand in all the unexpected blessings day after day. Please know that in every situation there are two stories: There's my story and perception, and then there's always His story—the part of the situation that gives us a bird's-eye view. His story gives us a purposeful view and shows us the Lord's amazing work in every situation of our lives. Please never forget: There is always another side to your story. His story has the best ending!

C3॰80

C3 relax

# His Conclusion

*CSFor I know the plans I have for you," declares the*
*Lord, "plans to prosper you and not to harm you,*
*plans to give you a hope and a future.*

*Jeremiah 29:11* (NIV)

C3 relax

# References:

http://www.negrospirituals.com/news-song/free_at_last_from.htm

http://www.azlyrics.com/lyrics/rkelly/ibelieveicanfly.html

http://www.allgospellyrics.com

www.ingramcontent.com/pod-product-compliance
Lightning Source LLC
Chambersburg PA
CBHW070546030426
42337CB00016B/2380